I0472371

Rights

Without

Obligation

Benefits of the overseas country and territory of the EU member's states and their compatibility with the principles of competition

Spiro Paço

ISBN: 9781095767641

CONTENTS

ABREVATIONS

CA2006   Companies Act 2006

EU   European Union

UK   United Kingdom

ECJ   European Court of Justice

EU   European Union

OCT   Overseas Countries and Territories

TEU   Treaty of European Union

TFEU   Treaty on the Functioning of the European Union

1 INTRODUCTION

The twenty one overseas countries and Territories depend constitutionally on four of the European Union Member States: Denmark, France, the Netherlands, and the United Kingdom. This OCT nationals are European citizens and for this reason enjoy all EU rights but the OCT are not automatically EU territory and EU law application is not 100% obligatory. [1]

However, these countries do not form part of EU territory. Accordingly, they are not directly subject to EU law, but they benefit from associate status conferred on them by the Treaty of Lisbon. The aim of this association is principally to contribute to their economic and social development. They profit from any advantage an EU territory have like grants and economic aid. [2]

---

[1] The Maastricht Treaty of 1992 (Treaty on European Union): Declaration on the outermost regions of the Community
[2] "Treaty of Lisbon, Article 2, points 287 and 293". Retrieved 15 January 2016.

Acording to EU website the legal definition of the OCT is[3]:

> """The OCTs are 25 countries and territories, which have special links with Denmark, France, the Netherlands and the United Kingdom and which are associated with the Union according to the provisions of the Treaty on the Functioning of the European Union. The relation between the EU and the OCTs is a function of the EU law, not of the constitutional law of the Member State [example: Saint-Pierre et Miquelon was previously an overseas department under French constitutional law, but has always been considered an OCT under EU law (and not an Outermost region)]. Their nationals are in principle EU citizens."""

Some EU member States have territory situated overseas divided in different category. The application of EU Company Law in this territory will be the focus of my paper. According to Article 52 of the TEU the EU treaties apply to the 28 Member States mentioned therefore. In accordance with this to all the dependences of the member states too. [4] The EU Law applies, in principle, to the whole territory of those Member States including the overseas parts of their territory without importance how fare from homeland they are. In Article 355 TFEU, the territorial scope of the treaties of EU is further specified. There are more or less three categories of territorial entity with regard to the overseas. [5]

---

[3] The Kingdom of the Netherlands: One Kingdom - Four Countries; European and Caribbean)". Ministerie van Buitenlandse Zaken. April 2015.

[4] "EU relations with Overseas Countries and Territories". European Commission. 4 June 2014.

[5] "Protocol: Setting out the fishing opportunities and financial contribution provided for in the Fisheries Partnership Agreement between the European

The first are the Outermost Regions where the law of EU applies, with the possibility for temporary exceptions to the acquis of the EU although the term 'temporary' is perhaps not the right word, since the derogations are constantly extended in this territory. The Outermost Regions consist in the French départements d'outre-mer, the Spanish Canary Islands and the Portuguese Azores and Madeira. [6]

Legal framework of the OCT Association according to European Union is[7]:

o   The establishment of close economic relations between the EU and the OCTs as a whole, amongst others through an improvement of the trade arrangements;

o   The promotion of EU's values, standards and interests in the wider world via the OCTs;

o   The enhancement of OCTs' competitiveness;

o   The strengthening of OCTs' resilience and reduction of their vulnerability;

o   The establishment of a more reciprocal relationship between EU and OCTs based on mutual interests and shared values;

o   The promotion of cooperation of OCTs with third partners.

Community (1) on the one hand, and the Government of Denmark and the Home Rule Government of Greenland (2), on the other hand" (PDF). Official Journal of the European Union. 23 October 2012.

[6] Outermost regions, Fact Sheets on the European Union, European Parliament.

[7] The OCT-EU Association is based on Articles 198 to 204 of Part IV of the Treaty on the Functioning of the European Union (TFEU)

Secondly the Overseas Countries and Territories (OCT) , where the law of EU applies, with the possibility for more permanent exceptions to the acquis of the Union. On the OCTs a special regime of EU-law is applicable: the association regime (of Part IV of the TFEU). The OCTs are listed in Annex II to the TFEU and consist of Danish Greenland, the French territories' and collectivités d'outre-mer, the Caribbean part of the Netherlands and most of 12 British Overseas Territories. [8]

And thirdly, custom made regimes for specific parts of some Member States, such as the Channel Islands and Åland Islands.   In addition some custom made regimes can be found in the accessions treaties, such as Gibraltar and the Spanish territories Ceuta and Mellila, which are situated on the African continent. [9]

This territory benefit from the EU citizenship and fundamental right. A citizen of Greenland holds automatically a Danish passport on request and enjoys all European Union rights. The citizen of all OCT benefits from all European advantages not only the four rights. These rights without obligation have lead to the transformation of this territory's to a sort of fiscal paradise. In the other hand the OCT have no fiscal obligation to EU institution like European Bank. [10]

---

[8] P. Craig & G. de Búrca, EU Law: Text, Cases and Materials (4th edn OUP 2008)
[9] Article 6 of Council Directive 2006/112/EC of 28 November 2006 (as amended) on the common system of value added tax
[10] "COUNCIL DECISION 2014/137/EU of 14 March 2014: On relations between the European Union on the one hand, and Greenland and the Kingdom of Denmark on the other" (PDF). Official Journal of the European Union

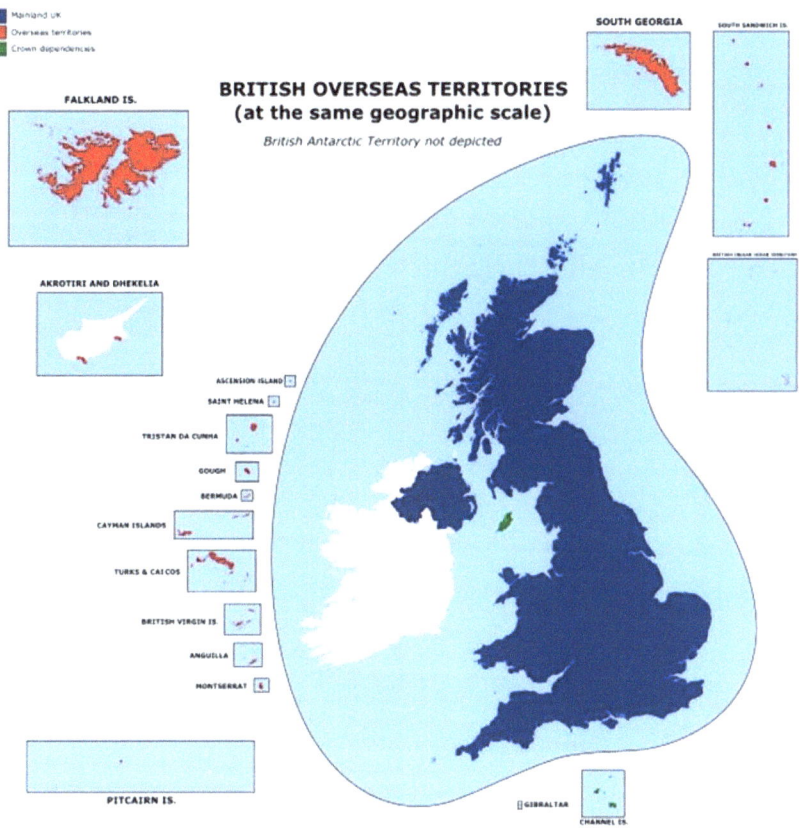

2 COMPETITION LAW IN THE EU OVERSEAS COUNTRIES AND TERRITORIES

In 2009, in a case concerning the market for mobile telecom on the French Indian Ocean islands of la Réunion and Mayotte, the French competition authority imposed interim measures on a subsidiary of the French telecom operator SFR because of (alleged) abuse of a dominant position; I use the word 'alleged', since the final decision is not given yet (cf. a second interim decision of 24 January 2012, par. 73 and 74). La Réunion is an Outermost Region and Mayotte an OCT. Concerning the question whether the behavior of SFR's subsidiary might also constitute an infringement of Article 102 TFEU, the French competition authority concluded the following: [11]

---

[11] Council Directive 2013/61/EU of December 2013" . 17 December 2013.

"La collectivité départementale de Mayotte est une collectivité territorial française qui ne fait pas partie de la Communauté européenne. Les dispositions du Traité CE ne lui sont donc pas applicables."

With regard to the two main categories Outermost Regions and OCT, the question arises whether Competition law of EU applies there or not. It is well established case law of the ECJ that the Outermost Regions constitute an integral part of the internal market. The OCTs are not part of the internal market and are therefore in a comparable situation as third countries. [12]

Since the decentralized enforcement of Competition law of EU, especially the French competition authority, l'Autorité de la concurrence, is confronted with that question, because the French republic incorporates both categories: Outermost Regions and OCTs. Some recent decisions of the French competition authority and in the aftermath of those decisions, the French courts, can answer our question. [13]

The following may be considered to be compatible with the internal market[14]:

---

[12] Judgments of the Court in Cases C-145/04 and C-300/04: Kingdom of Spain v United Kingdom of Great Britain and Northern Ireland, and M.G. Eman and O.B. Sevinger v College van burgemeester en wethouders van Den Haag
[13] "La collectivité de Saint-Barthélémy obtient un nouveau statut européen". Ministère de l'Outre-Mer (in French).
[14] "Schurende rechtsordes: Over juridische implicaties van de UPG-status voor de eilandgebieden van de Nederlandse Antillen en Aruba (Rijksuniversiteit Groningen)"

"(a) aid to promote the economic development of areas where the standard of living is abnormally low or where there is serious underemployment, and of the regions referred to in Article 349, in view of their structural, economic and social situation;

(b) aid to promote the execution of an important project of common European interest or to remedy a serious disturbance in the economy of a Member State;

(c) aid to facilitate the development of certain economic activities or of certain economic areas, where such aid does not adversely affect trading conditions to an extent contrary to the common interest;

(d) aid to promote culture and heritage conservation where such aid does not affect trading conditions and competition in the Union to an extent that is contrary to the common interest;

(e) such other categories of aid as may be specified by decision of the Council on a proposal from the Commission."

According to the French competition authority and the European Commission Competition law of the EU is thus applicable on the Outermost Regions and not on the OCTs. This is in my view not only the logic of Article 355 TFEU, but also of the concept that Outermost Regions are part on the internal market in which undistorted competition must be guaranteed by Competition law of the EU. The Commission came to the same conclusion with regard to the applicability of the state aid rules of Article 107 TFEU et seq. [15]

That was the main argument made by France Télécom and Orange Caraïbe when they appealed against a decision of the French competition authority which had fined them for abusing their dominant positions. France Télécom abused its dominant position on the French Antilles and French Guyana market for fixed telecom by offering low-cost tariffs for fixed-to-mobile telephone calls on its fixed and mobile networks when a new operator arrived on the market for mobile telecom. [16]

Can behavior on remote and isolated islands affect trade between Member States? Even though formally EU-Competition law applies to the Outermost Regions, it is very questionable whether inter-state trade can be affected by undertakings on the Outermost Regions since the overseas regions are suffering from remoteness and insular isolation. Without affect on inter-state trade, EU-Competition law remains inapplicable. [17]

---

[15] Articles 349 and 355 of the Treaty on the Functioning of the European Unio
[16] Article 200(1) [ex Article 184(1)]
[17] Art.198 of the EURATOM Treaty states that the treaty applies to non European territories under jurisdiction of Member States. So far there is no reference for Macau exclusion, thus considering it included between 1986 and

Orange Caraïbe had abused its dominant position on the French Antilles and French Guyana market for mobile telecom by several exclusive practices, such as exclusivity clauses for its independent distributors in those regions and loyalty 'rebates' for its customers, by offering mobile phones for free with long term contracts. The French competition authority considered this to be a breach of Article 102 TFEU, next to the breach of national competition law. [18]

In the Antilles-Guyana market for mobile telecom only one non-French operator was active; it was a Jamaican operator. The fined operators therefore put forward the argument that the possibility of effect on inter-state trade was theoretical, since no other EU-operators than French operators were active on the relevant market. The Paris Court of Appeal ruled that inter-state effect was theoretical and not proven. Consequently there was no breach of Article 102 TFEU. All parties appealed to the Cour de cassation, the French Supreme Court. The Commission intervened as an amicus curiae in this case on the basis of Article 15(3) Reg. 1/2003. [19]

The French Supreme Court decided that the Paris Court of Appeal erred in law, by accepting the argument that there was no other EU operator active or willing to be active on the relevant market and thereby there was no effect on inter-state trade. The foreclosure of the market by the French

1999.

[18] Article 3(1) of Council Regulation 2913/92/EEC of 12 October 1992 establishing the Community Customs Code (as amended) (OJ L 302, 19.10.1992, p. 1-50)

[19] Future relations between the EU and the Overseas Countries and Territories (PDF). Brussels: Commission of the European Communities. 25 May 2008.

operators could already be enough to conclude that there was effect on inter-state trade. The case has been sent back to the Paris Court of Appeal to a chamber with other judges than those who ruled earlier in this case in order to come to a final decision. [20]

What this case in my view demonstrates is that even though EU-Competition law formally applies in the Outermost Regions, it is questionable whether anti-competitive behavior by undertakings on the Outermost Regions can affect inter-state trade, because the Outermost Regions are remote and isolated islands. This is a factual analysis which has to be made on a case by case basis and depends of the market concerned.[21]

---

[20] "Consultative powers of the European Court of Auditors". CVCE. Retrieved 28 April 2013.
[21] The Maastricht Treaty of 1992 (Treaty on European Union): Declaration on the outermost regions of the Community

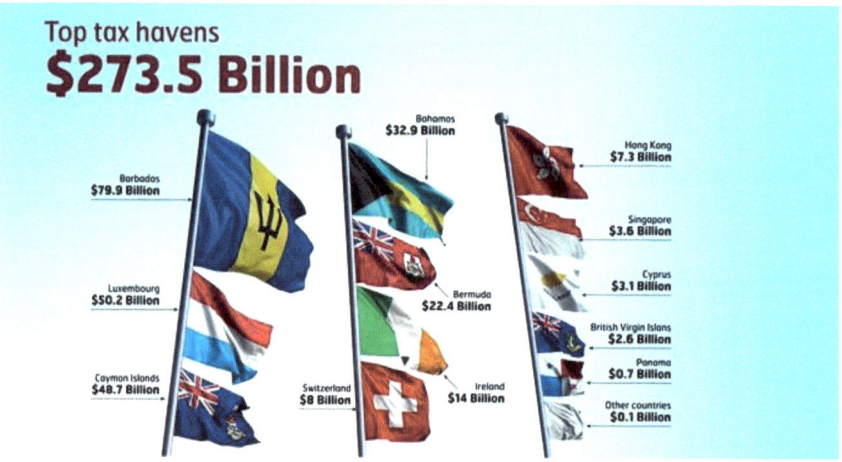

3 SHOULD COMPANY DIRECTORS HAVE A DUTY TO THEIR COMPANIES TO ENSURE THAT THEY AVOID PAYING TAX?

The principal goal of a company is to generate wealth and secure the continuation of this wealth this wealth must not be distributed only between the owner but also with the community through paying tax to the state. Economic journal and magazine are full of articles that deal with tax avoidance by big company. But is this a problem and if yes is a big problem? Yes the avoidance of payng tax is a big problem for the state, the community and the company itself considering that our economy is an immense chain.[22]

Today, 10 May 2013, that is in fact the deadline of the submersion of my peeper, a very entrusting thing happened and obligated me to change nearly

---

[22] ane G. Gravelle (2015). Tax Havens: International Tax Avoidance and Evasion. Congressional Research Service. ISBN 978-1482527681

all my paper. In the eave of the G-8 2013 summit that will be hold in London a group of person protest outside the office of George Osborne, the Chancellor of the Exchequer and Second Lord of the treasure of the UK. The protesters says: "UK TAX HEAVENS: THE ELEPHANT IN THE ROOM". This strange English metaphorical idiom for an obvious truth that is being ignored obligated me to see the situation in a different perspective.[23]

For nearly a month I try to right this paper supporting the idea that a "BIG ONE" company like Starbucks, Amazon or Google have not only the right but the duty to avoid paying tax using mechanism like tax heaven. But investigating in the social consequences that this have I change my mind.[24]

In the paper I will analyze the different and contemporaneous dilemma on tax avoidance and the different shareholders theory. From the 1970's Anglo-American jurisdiction shareholders theory to the most recent Company Act of 1985 and 2006. An important part of the paper will be also the differences of shareholders and stakeholders.[25]

As the most important part of the paper will be the explanation of the

---

[23] Nicholas Shaxson (2011). Treasure Islands: Uncovering the Damage of Offshore Banking and Tax Havens. Palgrave Macmillan. ISBN 978-0-230-10501
[24] Ronen Palan; Richard Murphy; Christian Chavagneux (2009). Tax Havens: How Globalization Really Works. Cornell University Press. ISBN 978-0-8014-7612-9.
[25] Raymond W. Baker (2005). Capitalism's Achilles' Heel: Dirty Money, and How to Renew the Free-Market System. John Wiley & Sons. ISBN 978-0471644880.

different case of tax avoidance and the consequences that this thing have. A special part of the paper will be also the Delaware Case as a specific case of great interest because created the precedent that permit the avoidance of paying tax if is not illegal.[26]

---

[26] Gabriel Zucman (2016). The Hidden Wealth of Nations: The Scourge of Tax Havens. University of Chicago Press. ISBN 978-0226422640.

4 COMPANIES ACT OF 2006: DIRECTORS DUTIES

The Company Law of a state can be considered one of its most important law that function and efficacy is viable for the general welfare . The UK as one of the biggest economy in the world with a global distribution, heritage of the British Colonial Empire, and home of great company like British Petroleum, Vodafone, British American Tobacco, Lloyds BG (... etc) needed a contemporaneous and updated Company Law. [27]

The Law of 1985 was unable to deal with the new problems and need of companies and society and was inevitable its substitution. Things like the directors duties and the inexistence of protection for stakeholder rise then necessity of change.   In 2006 a new Company Law was approved and entered into force. Parts of the old Company Act was introduced in the

---

[27] Scevola, Carlo; Sneiderova, Karina (January 2010). Offshore Jurisdictions Guide. Geneva, Switzerland: CS&P Fiduciaire. ISBN 978-1-60594-433-3.

new one but also many other thing where added reflecting the actual need of the market. [28]

An important point of the new Law was the improvement of company governance defined by point from 171 to 177 of the CA2006. As in the old law the Directors where obligated to operate under the company CA2006 of incorporation. Section 174 of the CA2006 describe the duties of the Directors and the fundamental personal skill they must have. Things like the general knowledge or the needed education and management experience become now very important and a real mean of selection of the directors. [29]

The new CA2006 also developed the idea of "company" from a propriety with profit and obligation only to the shareholders to a whole structure as interest of all its participant, shareholders and stakeholder. This was expressed in section 172 of the CA2006 also including a rise in the Directors term and giving perspective to a more successful work granting him a longer term. [30]

Important is to mention the duties of director to avoid any conflict of interest that can, voluntarily or not voluntarily, damage the company but

---

[28] Morriss, Andrew P. (2010). Offshore Financial Centers and Regulatory Competition. Washington: The AEI Press. ISBN 978-0-8447-4324-0.
[29] Foremny, D., & Von Hagen, J. (2012). "Fiscal federalism in times of crisis", CEPR Discussion Papers 9154, C.E.P.R. Discussion Papers.
[30] Micklethwait, John, and Adrian Wooldridge. 2003. The company: A short history of a revolutionary idea. New York: Modern Library.

according to the 2006 Act there is no specification on tax avoidance ban or limitation. In the section 176 of the CA2006 the Director is obligated not to accepted benefit from third parties but with special reference to transaction or arrangement with interest for him. [31]

---

[31] L Sealy and S Worthington, Cases and Materials in Company law (9th edn OUP, Oxford 2010)

5 DELAWARE CASE
AND HOW A FLEXIBLE CORPORATE TAX CAN INFLUENCE IN A COUNTRY?

According to the Company Act of 2006 Directors are free to avoid tax if this is not illegal. A simple explanation is that if something is not illegal it is legal. The Delaware Law Case is related to a court decision in Delaware where XTO company have been absolved for the accuse of   tax evasion. XTO played all obligatory tax and avoid the non mentioned obligatory other taxes. the corut decidet that can't punish a company for not doing something that is not binding and not illegal.   [32]

A similar decision have been given in the Seinfeld v Republic Services & Directors case. The case was simple, Directors give themselves lots of un taxable bonuses. In this whey they avoid paying tax and absorbed nearly all

---

[32] "Delaware General Corporation Law". Delaware Code Online.

the income of the company. The court normally didn't punish them for doing something not illegal and the case was closed. [33]

In this two cases we can se that not paying tax if is not obligatory by low is not a problem but we will se in the other part of the paper that this thing have consequences.[34]

"In Venezuela Chavez has made the co-ops a top political priority, giving them first refusal on government contracts and offering them economic incentives to trade with one another. By 2006, there were roughly 100,000 co-operatives in the country, employing more than 700,000 workers. Many are pieces of state infrastructure – toll booths, highway maintenance, health clinics – handed over to the communities to run.

It's a reverse of the logic of government outsourcing – rather than auctioning off pieces of the state to large corporations and losing democratic control, the people who use the resources are given the power to manage them, creating, at least in theory, both jobs and more responsive public services.

Chavez's many critics have derided these initiatives as handouts and unfair subsidies, of course. Yet in an era when Halliburton treats the U.S. government as its personal ATM for six years, withdraws upward of $20

---

[33] Gullifer and Payne Corporate Finance Law: Principles and Policy (2nd Edn Hart Publishing, 2015)
[34] Feldman, Sandra (17 May 2017). "Choice of Entity for Startups Seeking Venture Capital". Wolters Kluwer. CT Corporation System.

billion in Iraq contracts alone, refuses to hire local workers either on the

Gulf coast or in Iraq, then expresses its gratitude to U.S. taxpayers by moving its corporate headquarters to Dubai (with all the attendant tax and legal benefits), Chavez's direct subsidies to regular people look significantly less radical."

— Naomi Klein[35]

There is a general debate over what the basic duties of Directors and a Company as a whole. Shareholder theories of the company argue that businesses have a primary duty to their shareholders, to maximize the value of their shares and a primary duty to enrich their communities.[36]

Supporters of the stakeholder theory believe that the company own its profit from the community and have a duty to redistribute the wealth they generate . If the community is impoverished there will be problem also in the company within that community, and so there is also a justification for stakeholder theory from self-interest. [37]

Supporters of the shareholder theory make their case on the basis of the different functions that company can fulfill. The company are created in

---

[35] The Shock Doctrine: The Rise of Disaster Capitalism. Knopf Canada. ISBN 978-0676978001 (2007)

[36] The Way to Wealth. CreateSpace Independent Publishing Platform. ISBN 978-1532945083

[37] Tideman, Sander G. (2016), Gross National Happiness: Lessons for Sustainability Leadership, South Asian Journal of Global Business Research

order to generate wealth. They do this by seeking the maximum profits available for themselves and that can then be passed on to their shareholders. Other functions of company can be best fulfilled by other kinds of company, such as non-profits and government agencies.[38]

Both shareholder theory and stakeholder theory primarily deal with the internal deliberation that company go through when considering their primary goal. Government regulation is meant to impose obligation on company from the outside. Shareholder theory and stakeholder theory have great influence in the government regulation, however, in the sense that the duties of a company owes others shape what you feel they should be compelled to do. Regulation often imposes both shareholder and stockholder duties on businesses.[39]

---

[38] Watterson, Juliana M.: Corporation Tax 2009/2010, Bloomsbury Professional, ISBN 978-1-84766-327-6
[39] Kahn & Lehman. Corporate Income Taxation

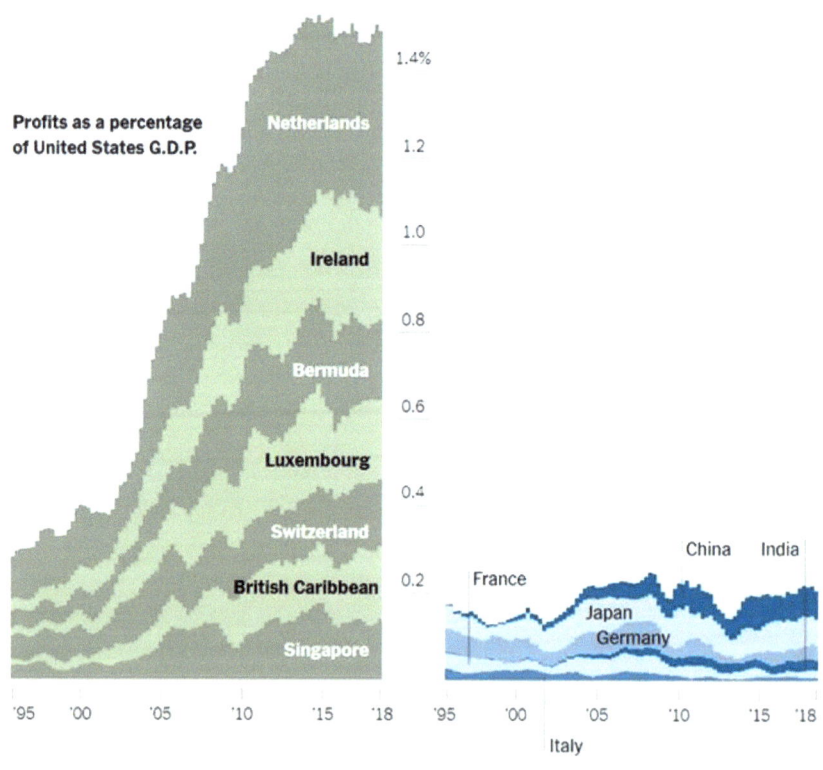

6 SHAREHOLDERS THEORY AND SHAREHOLDERS PROTECTION

The shareholders Theory or Shareholder primacy is a theory in corporate Law that promote the idea that shareholder interests is a priority. The shareholder primacy often gives shareholders the power to interfere openly and regularly in corporate direction. This means that the shareholder have the power to modify corporate articles. [40]

"If private property were truly respected, shareholder interest would be the primary, or even better, the sole purpose, of the corporation."

The doctrine of shareholder primacy is sometimes criticized for being at odds with corporate social responsibility and other legal obligations. The

---

[40] LA Bebchuk, JC Coates and G Subramanian, "The Powerful Antitakeover Force of Staggered Boards: Theory, Evidence, and Policy" (2002) 54(5) Stanford Law Review. JSTOR 1229689.

Shareholders Theory normally is in favor of shareholders but it also can be considered in favor of the company if we consider the company only a propriety of the shareholder. [41]

Is simple to understand the benefit of this theory. If the company made profit they will go to the shareholder and if the company don't made profit will be the shareholders that will lose their interest. In contrast to the possible profit or economic loss the shareholder in this theory have the possibility to be active in the decisions that will be taken so they will be personally responsible for the outcome of this decision. Considering their financial interest we can understand that the decision will be fully in accordance with the interest of the company. [42]

We have to discus also on the negative aspect of this theory. The shareholder maybe do not have the necessary skill to take the decision and also thy are not daily informed about the company state. The shareholder can be employed in anather company and don;t have the time to be present in evry decision and many other reason this theory have its gaps but still is used for its good parts. [43]

---

[41] Wachtell, Lipton, Rosen & Katz, The Share Purchase Rights Plan in Ronald J. Gilson & Bernard S. Black, "The Law and Finance of Corporate Acquisitions" (2d ed. Supp. 1999)

[42] Ross, Westerfield, Jordan & Roberts, Fundamentals of Corporate Finance (6th ed. McGraw-Hill Ryerson) : "Mergers and Acquisitions"

[43] See Bebchuk, Lucian; Coates, John C.; Subramanian, Guhan (2002). "The Powerful Antitakeover Force of Staggered Boards: Theory, Evidence, and Policy". Stanford Law Review.

"Andorra, the Bahamas, Belize, Bermuda, the British Virgin Islands, the Cayman Islands, the Channel Islands, the Cook Islands, Hong Kong, the Isle of Man, Mauritius, Lichtenstein, Monaco, Panama, Switzerland and St. Kitts and Nevis are all considered tax havens. However, pressure from foreign governments that want to collect all the tax revenue they believe they are entitled to has caused some tax haven countries to sign tax information exchange agreements (TIEAs) and mutual legal assistance treaties (MLAT) that provide foreign governments with formerly secret information about investors' offshore accounts. A "Tax Heaven" is a country that offers foreign individuals and businesses little or no tax liability in a politically and economically stable environment. Tax havens also provide little or no financial information to foreign tax authorities. Individuals and businesses that do not reside a tax haven can take advantage of these countries' tax regimes to avoid paying taxes in their home countries. Tax havens do not require that an individual reside in or a business operate out of that country in order to benefit from its tax policies."[44]

We now that many great company now are offshore company, established in tax heaven or offshore financial center with nearly full tax exemption.

The general opinion is that a tax heaven can be considered a small island in the pacific when the millionaires put their money but this is not true. Every country that have a lower taxation then the home country can be

---

[44] Raymond W. Baker (2005). Capitalism's Achilles' Heel: Dirty Money, and How to Renew the Free-Market System. John Wiley & Sons. ISBN 978-0471644880.

---

considered advantageous. For Starbucks, Google or Amazon is not need to transfer their company in an isolated island. Today there are an immense number of state that give good opportunities to pay lass tax. You have no need to go outside Europe. Microstate inside Europe like Luxembourg, Liechtenstein or even bigger like Ireland offer lower tax then the UK. There are also parts inside the UK that have a lower tax duty like the Channel Island, Isle of Man or the famous Cayman Island and Bermuda.[45]

> "If you make any money, the government shoves you in the creek once a year with it in your pockets, and all that don't get wet you can keep."
>
> - Will Rogers[46]

So if a great company in accordance with the law avoid paying allot of tax in the UK and pay a symbolic sum to this Tax Heaven is this a good or bed thing?[47]

Pros: We can consider this a good think because now the company have more money that can be spent to make it bigger or distributed to the shareholders and stakeholders increasing their personal wealth. [48]

---

[45] Ronen Palan; Richard Murphy; Christian Chavagneux (2009). Tax Havens: How Globalization Really Works. Cornell University Press. ISBN 978-0-8014-7612-9.

[46] Gabriel Zucman (2016). The Hidden Wealth of Nations: The Scourge of Tax Havens. University of Chicago Press. ISBN 978-0226422640.

[47] Foremny, D., & Von Hagen, J. (2012). "Fiscal federalism in times of crisis", CEPR Discussion Papers 9154, C.E.P.R. Discussion Papers.

[48] Henry, James S. (October 2003). The Blood Bankers: Tales from the Global Underground Economy. New York, NY: Four Walls Eight Windows. ISBN 978-1-

Cons: In the other hand the avoidance of paying tax have many bad consequences. We have to consider the source of this wealth. The company sell its product generally in the UK we can say that the company collect the wealth of the people of the UK and not paying tax the source will be exhaust after some time. I consider the economy like a big chain and the money as the ring of the chain. If a company avoid paying taxes in practice is limiting the number of rings in the chain thing that make the economy more fragile. [49]

Also the government will have lass money if great company avoid paying tax. Las money mean lass investment in infrastructure, research, education, security that one day like a boomerang will transformed to a great problem for the company itself.[50]

> "A democracy cannot exist as a permanent form of government. It can only exist until the people discover they can vote themselves largess out of the public treasury. From that moment on, the majority always votes for the canidate promising the most benefits from the public treasury, with the result that democracy always collapses over a loose fiscal policy--to be followed by a dictatorship."
>
> — Alexander Fraser Tytler[51]

56858-254-2.
[49] Alan Rusbridger (27 October 2016). "Panama: The Hidden Trillions" (part 1 of 2), The New York Review of Books
[50] Morriss, Andrew P. (2010). Offshore Financial Centers and Regulatory Competition. Washington: The AEI Press. ISBN 978-0-8447-4324-0.
[51] The Complete Works of Robert Burns (Self-Interpreting), Volume IV, Gebbie

So paying lass tax is possible and to some extent legal but can have very bad consequences. A believe that the solution of this dilemma will be a middle chaise. The company will never pay more then they are obligated to pay by law and this obligate the state to be more flexible in tax law. I believe is important to balance the goal of the company to generate wealth with the obligation to pay tax. [52]

Have the Directors the duty to avoid tax if possible? Again the same question. And I'm again confused. Lets do a simple reasoning. The directors are high skilled employed person. They have to do what is the better for the company. The company have as its goal the generation of wealth. Avoiding tax normally will make the company benefit from this and we can say that tax avoidance by the Director is exactly what should they do.[53]

But generally the tax are imposed over en income and company that didn't earn money will not have to pay to many taxes or will not pay at all. So I believe that if a company generate a profit have to pay for the commune development.[54]

& Co., Philadelphia (1886)

[52] Minarik, Joseph J. (2008). "Taxation". In David R. Henderson (ed.) (ed.). Concise Encyclopedia of Economics (2nd ed.). Library of Economics and Liberty. ISBN 978-0865976658.

[53] Kerr, Gavin (10 March 2015). "'Predistribution', property-owning democracy and land value taxation'". 'Politics, Philosophy and Economics"

[54] Slack, E., & Bird, R. M. (2014). The Political Economy of Property Tax Reform, OECD Working Papers on Fiscal Federalism 18, OECD Publishing.

This paper was rally interesting and the collection of materials was not difficult considering that internet is full of journal articles and online Scand book that deal with this question. As i see this topic was very discussed and many ideas where given. Tax avoidance in general is a great problem of developed states and specifically the UK. After 2006 the UK have a new Company Act that is really simplified and efficient but that live a great enigma on our question.[55]

Our response to this question is that yes in the interest of the company the Director can and must avoid paying tax but only in the case where this in not forbidden by law.[56]

In my opinion Directors have the duty to ensure the financial development of the company and the distribution of the generated wealth to the shareholders. The CA 2006 is very clear in what the Director have and not have to do. The goal of the position of the Director of a Corporation is tu secure a great profit and the Directors of great Multi-National company like Google or Amazon have decided to avoid paying more tax then is obligatory by the law. Using offshore company in country like Luxemburg or Cyprus that with their being inside EU a and double taxation treaty offer a good possibility for this company to pay "lass" taxes.[57]

---

[55] Tolley's Corporation Tax, 2007-2008 ISBN 978-0-7545-3273-6

[56] Watterson, Juliana M.: Corporation Tax 2009/2010, Bloomsbury Professional, ISBN 978-1-84766-327-6

[57] Hoffman, et al.: Corporations, Partnerships, Estates and Trusts, ISBN 978-0-324-66021-0

As a conclusion I definitely, maybe unexpectedly, after analyzing the effect that the tax avoidance have in a society confirm that a Director have the duties to do what is in his power to pay lass but also avoid creating risk for the company.[58]

---

[58] Healy, John C. and Schadewald, Michael S.: Multistate Corporate Tax Course 2010, CCH, ISBN 978-0-8080-2173-5 (also available as a multi-volume guide, ISBN 978-0-8080-2015-8)

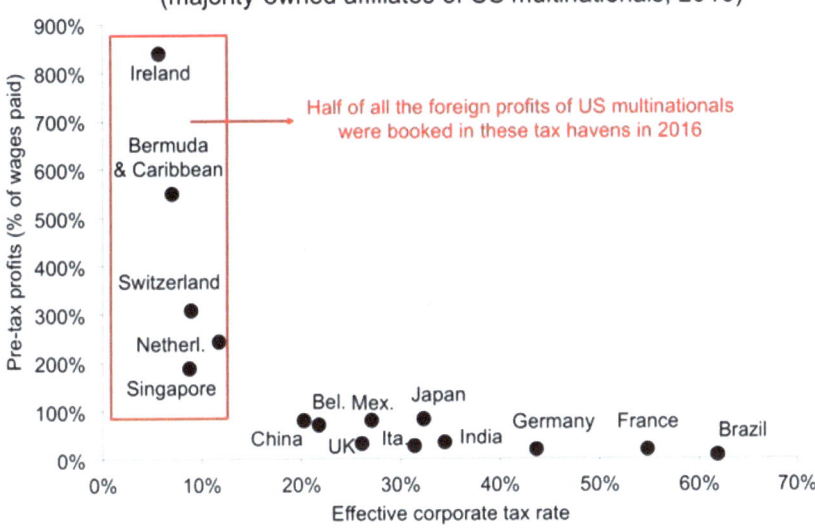

Where do US multinationals book their profits?
(majority-owned affiliates of US multinationals, 2016)

7 HAVE THE DIRECTORS THE DUTY TO AVOID PAYING TAX?

The EU member state as consequence of historical factor conserve peace of territory fare from homeland. These have affected EU in many ways but the financial damage and the break of equality and fair trading may have bad consequences. In the last years millions of EU citizens and great EU Company have change residence in this OCT. [59]

The case of French Court Judging the violation of fair trade and competition in the French Antilles is only one of the many cases in witch EU Courts (Paris Court in this case) have sentenced Company that abused by fvors created to the OCT.[60]

---

[59] Kahn & Lehman. Corporate Income Taxation
[60] Bittker, Boris I. and Eustice, James S.: Federal Income Taxation of Corporations and Shareholders: paperback ISBN 978-0-7913-4101-8

To the question if there are violation of fair trade and competition in the OCT I can respond that in all the official documents of the EU that I analyze is seen evident that in the OCT will be abuses with competition but this is seen as a help for economic development of the dependences. Officially this territory avoid paying obligation to the central government like all other homeland region do, in this way we can say that they avoid also their economic duty toward the EU. [61]

On the other hand the OCT benefit from EU development programs or direct economic aid. Is important to mention that most of the OCT products do not have custom duty to pay entering EU considered as internal market but have the right to impose custom duty to EU products only by considering to avoid any national discrimination.[62]

Many scholar have give as a solution for this problems the obligation of the OCT to decide between independence or full national integration. In similar case both the outcome have ménage to be successful. The best example is the French Guyana that is by many years integral part of French Republic and is the South American territory with highest GDP per capita. Its citizen enjoy only Frensh citizenship and EU citizenship and have the same

---

[61] Clarke, Thomas & dela Rama, Marie (eds.) (2008) Fundamentals of Corporate Governance (4 Volume Series) London and Thousand Oaks, CA: SAGE, ISBN 978-1-4129-3589-0

[62] Erturk, Ismail, Froud, Julie, Johal, Sukhdev and Williams, Karel (2004) Corporate Governance and Disappointment Review of International Political Economy,

national and European rights and responsibility as any other Frenchman.[63]

This paper was rally interesting and the collection of materials was not difficult considering that internet is full of journal articles and online Scand book that deal with this question. As i see this topic was very discussed and many ideas where given. Tax avoidance in general is a great problem of developed states and specifically the UK. After 2006 the UK have a new Company Act that is really simplified and efficient but that live a great enigma on our question.[64]

Our response to this question is that yes in the interest of the company the Director can and must avoid paying tax but only in the case where this in not forbidden by law.[65]

In my opinion Directors have the duty to ensure the financial development of the company and the distribution of the generated wealth to the shareholders. The CA 2006 is very clear in what the Director have and not have to do. The goal of the position of the Director of a Corporation is tu secure a great profit and the Directors of great Multi-National company like Google or Amazon have decided to avoid paying more tax then is

---

[63] Low, Albert, 2008. "Conflict and Creativity at Work: Human Roots of Corporate Life, Sussex Academic Press. ISBN 978-1-84519-272-3

[64] Sun, William (2009), How to Govern Corporations So They Serve the Public Good: A Theory of Corporate Governance Emergence, New York: Edwin Mellen, ISBN 978-0-7734-3863-7.

[65] Dignam, A and Lowry, J (2006) Company Law, Oxford University Press ISBN 978-0-19-928936-3

obligatory by the law. Using offshore company in country like Luxemburg or Cyprus that with their being inside EU a and double taxation treaty offer a good possibility for this company to pay "lass" taxes.[66]

As a conclusion I definitely, maybe unexpectedly, after analyzing the effect that the tax avoidance have in a society confirm that a Director have the duties to do what is in his power to pay lass but also avoid creating risk for the company.[67]

---

[66] Clarke, Thomas (2007) "International Corporate Governance" London and New York: Routledge, ISBN 0-415-32309-6
[67] Brickley, James A., William S. Klug and Jerold L. Zimmerman, Managerial Economics & Organizational Architecture, ISBN

8 BIBLIOGRAPHY

Treaty on the Functioning of the European Union

Treaty of the European Union

Finnish accession treaty (OJ C 241, 29.08.1994) Protocol 2 (on the Åland Islands)

Act concerning the conditions of accession of the UK, Ireland and Denmark to the European Communities

Denise Matthews Case 1999

European Competition Network (ECN) Brief February 2012

Preliminary References to the European Court of Justice

Global Competition Review

Communication from the Commission

Commission publishes amicus curiae observations submitted to national courts

Application of Competition rules by national courts – Article 15 (3)

Commission observations to National Courts (Amicus curiae observations, Article 15(3))

Companies House function manual

Companies Act 1985

Companies Act 2006

Delaware State Courts

Susan Freedman v XTO & Board of directors, (2012), C.A. No. 4199-VCN

Seinfeld v. Republic Services & Directors,(2012), C.A. No.6462 VCG

The Multinational Challenge to Corporation Law: The Search for a New Corporate Personality, (1993) Blumberg, Phillip I.

"Shareholder Definitions: Profusion and Confusion" Miles, Samantha (2011).

The Ethical Corporation? James Kee (May 1995)

Shareholders: Theory and Practice. Oxford University Press. Friedman, Andrew L. and Samantha Miles.

Shareholder Theory, State of the Art, Cambridge University Press, 2010 Freeman, Harrison, Wicks, Parmar and De Colle,

Multistakeholder Processes for Governance and Sustainability: Beyond Deadlock and Conflict. Hemmati, Minu; et al. (2002).

Offshore Financial Centers and Regulatory Competition. Washington: The AEI Press

BakerCapitalism's Achilles' Heel: Dirty Money, and How to Renew the Free-Market System. Hoboken, New Jersey: John Wiley & Sons. , Raymond W. (August 2005). Morriss, Andrew P. (2010).

BakerCapitalism's Achilles' Heel: Dirty Money, and How to Renew the Free-Market System. Hoboken, New Jersey: John Wiley & Sons. , Raymond W. (August 2005).

ABOUT THE AUTHOR

LL.M. Spiro Paço is currently Director of the Department of Curricula and Quality Standards at "Aleksandër Moisiu" University, Durres, Albania. He has completed Bachelor studies in "Law" with excellent results at "Luarasi" University College and "Master" (LL.M.) studies at the University of Greenwich in "International and Commercial Law".

Mr. Paço is a member of the National Chamber of Advocates in the Republic of Albania.

He has conducted various trainings in Albanian and EU Institutions on topics such as: Constitutional Law; EU and US institutions; Prevention of Money Laundering and Terrorism Financing; World history; geopolitical; Migration issues; Theoretical Issues on Governance Systems etc.

Mr. Paço is a participant in several scientific conferences at home and abroad and in many projects of academic character. He has been engaged as Lawyer (Head of Legal Office, Head of Human Resources Office, Counselor) at some of the most well-known companies in Albania. He's Academic Engagement has started at the University of Durrës "Aleksandër Moisiu", as a lecturer of "Institution History" and " Environment Law" courses.

For two years he has been a part of the academic staff of the Luarasi University College, at the Public Department and has given his contribution as lecturer in the courses of "History of Institutions", "History of Law in Albania", "Constitutional Law", "Philosophy and Law".